CONTAINED IN ICE

LIZZIE FINCHAM

Cinnamon Press
:: small miracles from distinctive voices ::

Published by Cinnamon Press
www.cinnamonpress.com

The right of Lizzie Fincham to be identified as author of this work has been asserted by her in accordance with the Copyright, Designs and Patent Act, 1988. Copyright © 2020 Lizzie Fincham ISBN: 978-1-78864-090-9
British Library Cataloguing in Publication Data. A CIP record for this book can be obtained from the British Library.

Designed and typeset in Palatino by Cinnamon Press.
Cover design by Adam Craig.
Cinnamon Press is represented in the UK by Inpress Ltd and in Wales by the Books Council of Wales.

Acknowledgements

'Later we will dance' was First Prize Winner in the Brighton & Hove Competition, 2017 as 'Brexit Blues' and 'Paris Blues:Global Warning' was on the Poetry on the Lake Competition Longlist, 2019.

Contents

To Tula, Amiti, Theo, Jyoti, Aaditya
& their Climate Future

Contained in Ice

Specimen trays

At the edge of sleep
               open a specimen tray of the mind
                       stone masons hammering
                  chipping out gargoyles at the cathedral
            echoes and shadows dodging about

in all the houses of your life
and that door that was almost always shut

though once when she opened the door
        to the mewling cat you saw a glimpse
              of a courtyard
                strung with white sheets
                  transfigured in sunshine
      cadences of the flute polished as brass splashed out.

     You know the tune is familiar but   just out of reach.

Another memory is snagged by the click
of that latch by the corner of piled books
near the gate.   When the removal men leave
      these photos and paintings will change the energy
            of the new space.

Now, late in the day

     open a specimen drawer and you will find
        the Antarctic or even Galapagos laid out on a tray.

Later we will dance

…and so, with morning energy in mind
on the bus long before nine
I'm signing an on-line petition from Greenpeace
about pesticide use harming honey bees

seeing surf riding high across the empty beach
Sussex pretending to be Greece.
On this day
the sea has changed to a colder blue.

That couple on the balcony are probably still
eating peaches. Hospital workers
are speed-reading thrillers next to bank clerks
who have learned English all summer

as the bus takes twenty-one stops to get to the station
where the piano is being played
by the man with no shoes and the hands of an angel
jazzing up our Fridays.

Later we will dance.

By six in the Italian café across the road from the laundrette
the chef is coaxing rather shy English tomatoes into Italian warmth
with oil and basil although the man at the next table
who is boasting about his watch collection

and who is wearing a handful of diamonds
                    seems to have forgotten where he is
                         and is singing an eulogy to his Greek salad.
                                        Horiatiki, horiatiki, horiatiki!
The chef is too polite (or wise)
              to contradict him for a man with a watch
                   for every day of the year seems like a man who might
                        not   appreciate being challenged

about the correct terms for the still life on his plate.
                    And anyway perhaps the chef too loves
                              the sound of the Greek song.
                                        Horiatiki, horiatiki, horiatiki!

Contained in ice

Such a hasty leaving
grief peppering the walls of the first house.

There was a man once
in the blue room.
By a sea.

Contained in ice.
Reading between the lines.

Wild garlic is rampaging too early
in this spring cusping summer.
In the last house valerian spills.

From the bookshop meeting
      it was a hasty leaving
           near the visceral cathedral.
                  Contained in ice.

A few houses in that narrowest of narrow villages.
All occupied.   But not all lived in.

One book was left
on the threshold.

Waterhouse's cathedral

Five minutes' walk from the blue whale
we will meet in the Polish café today
at six o'clock.

        You will tell me about the hexagonal eyes
        of prawn larvae which square off, square up
        when they become adults.

As we crumble bread
and drink wine
I will tell you of that morning in Brighton
        in the church of St Mary Magdalene
        when the sound of men singing the mass in Polish
        was like a male voice choir in Wales.

A lament.

The glass-house window was broken

The glass-house window was broken.
Ice coated the vine.

World almost empty at ten that morning.
No-one waiting in the house by the weir.
Thirty minutes in the silent peacock garden.

Back from the visit
contained in ice
ninety mile beach and a day to spend.
Empty at six that morning.
The glass-house window was broken.

Ice coated the vine.
On the table the pages of his speech
were smeared with tears.

Moon white at eight that evening
through the apple tree.

Back from the visit, contained in ice
that girl was still playing her saxophone
and the mason was slicing marble again near the *kouros*.

Twenty minutes after the train had left

in the kitchen garden the lemon tree was filled with light bulbs.

Nine minutes. Then the plan changed.

In the glass-house the leaves unfurled as the sun broke through.
In the manor-house garden knives and forks smashed in the wind in the ash tree.

The sand was ribbed underfoot. Bladderwrack and *porphyra* in the rock pools.

The ferry was covered in ice.

One window on the orchard

Throughout our lands

Czesław Miłosz

another on the street scene in that strange house
straddling two worlds, the garden and the city.
(The house was tall and narrow
like a house in an old tale, the turret
of a castle or a watch-tower at a border.)

From each side, scenes slide under the moon, the stars
and the sun as more rain falls.
We run from window to window
to watch the world show up outside.
The guillotine is wheeled into the square again

where the street-cleaning machine is sluicing fresh blood
into the gutters. From the window over the garden
we can see how this August snow is already
weighing down apple trees in the orchard
and there are new boot prints on the earth.

Home, exile, return

Act One   Home

With Milosz, is it always quotidian nouns
that carry the weight
and freight of his words?
(Of course the poems are always in translation.)

Bed, table, chairs
in a hut or a house.
We notice similar objects
in folk museums

perhaps in Greece with an icon
and a rocking cradle,
in Wales with one cooking pot on the hearth,
a few bowls, spoons laid out

and in Poland that tall fire-place
decorated with blue tiles
a bed in a cupboard
and the broken slate of a child on the floor.

Act Two   Exile

Running or hiding
                in barns or in forests
                      beech-woods too dangerous
                                and fields over-looked

taking chances with strangers
                      a bed in the attic
                            a ride in the bone-cart
                                  rattle-cart.

What is your name?
Where are you from?
Where are you going?
Where are your papers?

The sludge of a river
the softest bed.
A boat docking at a jetty.
Treacherous steps.

Act Three   Return

It is the same place. It is not the same place.
(The poems are always in translation.)
The hut is occupied
                    the house is abandoned

the fields are deserted
                        the forest and beech-woods too full.
What is your name?
Where are you from?

Your accent is different.

Where are your papers?

Russian steppes

Perhaps these are the Russian steppes
                              snow fields stretching into the distance?
Wolves are howling under the lemon moon.
The bride is bare-headed
                    walking away across the snow.
Over her white frock she wears a scarlet coat.
She is walking alone.

From inside the Great Hall
the woman who has danced the polka
   (or was it the tango?) with Death
is watching the girl   walk further and further away towards the forest.

In the empty house by the weir
the pendulum swings faster
in the clock in the green-house

torn sheets of paper are lifted high above the desk
as the wind invades the room
sweeping across the tundra
where the wolves are skittering now under the moon.

There was a village once

We stopped at that village
                looking for coffee or ouzo perhaps
when we noticed the woman watching us from a doorway
holding a child close.

We saw few people came to this village.
No taverna.
Just a slice of a bar
and a ravine   dropping away behind the houses

huddled on the hill like the ones
in Carlo Levis's *Christ stopped at Eboli.*
The name of the village (if it had one) has long gone
but not the face of the woman

who needed to be wary of strangers.
And she had no reason to smile at us.

Snails

Woke above a bay turning from green into blue
white walls shocking in sunshine.
A gecko slipping out of sight.

> In the field the man woke too
> > shaking himself into morning.
> > > On moon nights he always slept outside.

We nodded a greeting, raised a hand most days.
Every few months his daughter came by,
scoured out his shack with buckets of soapy water
> which rivered onto paths
> > while ants re-directed their progress
> > seeking sweetness.

After she left his three blue shirts blew in the *meltemi,*
secured by pegs and out of reach
of even the boldest goats.

> The man (whose name was Jacob)
> > knew the best places for edible snails
> > > that appeared after rain showers.

Knew, too, the plants to eat in times of scarcity.
There are always fugitives in these hills
collecting survival
> paths to safety learned as children
> > when the world had torn itself apart
> > > once, twice, so many times before.

Paris Blues: Global Warning

I
have been
working at this table
for twenty, thirty days
this autumn while outside,
trees did what they had to do
fire-working from green to orange
then red as politicians strutted then fizzled
on the strumpet stage. In another gallery, Ravilious,
Caspar Friedrich, Manet give each other quiet courtesies of space,
their wintering skies waiting for our attention
to turn to a different Ice Age.

In a Field Station deep in Wytham Woods
some subtle variations suggest climate change.

Global Warming. Global Warning.
All the small stuff. All the big stuff.

Notching up

Before the end of March
clouds mine-sweep the fields
bending grasses
heads of sheep
in snow-storm blossom
from the blackthorn

barbed wire of the Saxons.
Ice saint winter scheduled for May
appears early this spring
up-ending country sayings
of times and seasons
as our foolish notching up

the thermostat of the earth
continues to bite.

The woods are turning

The woods are turning into the colour of smoke
as the working world changes its clocks
while men, women, children
      carry infants and possessions on their backs
      as the organised world gets ready to assess
      their papers, their languages, their tribes.

Woods are turning again into a pall of smoke
as the killing fleets slide through foreign waters
on the way to warm water ports
      where another Peter the Great will consolidate
      a stronghold, a stranglehold, where the cities have already turned
to the colour and texture of smoke

and across Europe groups will build more bonfires
bone-fires which seem to remember all our vicious histories
of terror and revenge as the figures will be dressed again
      in cardinals' robes, army camouflage, balaclavas and burkas
      as fresh walls of fear and suspicion are cemented into place
      at newer borders by politicians and other predators

while we are distracted by bread and circuses
      as though the fires in the camps
         are simply the stuff of old tales
            not the encampments of shelter
               as the woods are turning into smoke

There is no house

The Manor

Czesław Miłosz

But here is a rougher garden
where the house once sang.

The moon still bowls over the harbour
and although the window that framed it is smashed

the same wind blows the slanting rain
into the line strung with bleached sheets

though there is no line
there are no bleached sheets

now fennel gains ground over the lintel
and in the space which was once the house

the smells are doubled and re-doubled
as plants make free in the space.

The dogs still return to choose their shade
under the tree beside the wall

although there is now no wall.
As it always has, the bell tolls.

Created by hand

Created by hand over centuries, across countries
beyond the Silk Road, these buildings tried to reach
or mirror the sky with spires or domes

capturing space and candle-light
in an embrace of cold stone
or marble.

Buckets of water were hauled up onto planks of wood
stonemasons choosing stones as carefully as bread
through decades of time

as farmers still mend dry-stone walls
round the edges of ancient fields
marking boundaries

showing possession of territories
earth-bound
quibbling and quarrelling over rights of way

telling of old villainies
or new terrors
as if there is never enough

land or water, light or air to spare.

www.ingramcontent.com/pod-product-compliance
Lightning Source LLC
Chambersburg PA
CBHW032248070726
47590CB00017B/3117